ROBERT BISSELL'S

Rabbits and Be

COLORING BOOK

Growing up on a farm, Robert Bissell learned to love animals and nature. When he became a painter, he chose to make pictures of wild animals living in an enchanted land. The rabbits and bears in his paintings can do extraordinary things, like float a foot above the ground and tell each other stories. They seem to have a very peaceful, happy life in their magical world, and they all seem to be thinking about something, don't they?

This coloring book contains twenty line drawings of Robert Bissell's paintings for you to color. The full-color paintings are shown as small pictures on the inside front and back covers. When you color in the line drawings, you can copy the original colors or you can experiment with other color combinations of your own. You might color the bunnies and bears in shades of grey and brown, as they appear in nature, or you could make them bright primary colors or even neon colors.

We've left the last three pages of this coloring book blank so you can create your own animal pictures. Can you draw animals that look as wide-awake and curious about life as Robert Bissell's rabbits and bears?

Pomegranate publishes much more of Robert Bissell's artwork in the book *Hero: The Paintings of Robert Bissell* (2013).

Pomegranate Kids
AGES 3 to 103!

1. *The Swimmer* (detail), 2010. Oil on canvas, 121.9 x 91.4 cm (48 x 36 in.). Private collection.

2. *The Resolve,* 2009. Oil on canvas, 61 x 86.4 cm (24 x 34 in.). Private collection.

3. *Rangers,* 2009. Oil on canvas, 101.6 x 76.2 cm (40 x 30 in.). Private collection.

4. *Rhapsody,* 2007. Oil on linen, 76.2 x 116.8 cm (30 x 46 in.). Private collection.

5. *The Swimming Hole* (detail), 2009. Oil on canvas, 76.2 x 106.7 cm (30 x 42 in.). Private collection.

6. *The Dancers,* 2011. Oil on canvas, 91.4 x 76.2 cm (36 x 30 in.). Private collection.

7. *AM (#2),* 2010. Oil on canvas, 101.6 x 132.1 cm (40 x 52 in.). Collection of Gregory and Mary Jo Schiffman.

8. *The Crossing,* 2007. Oil on canvas, 76.2 x 66 cm (30 x 26 in.). Collection of Mary and Randy Kirst.

9. *The Story,* 2012. Oil on canvas, 106.7 x 101.6 cm (42 x 40 in.). Collection of the artist.

10. *The Dilemma,* 2003. Oil on canvas, 71.1 x 101.6 cm (28 x 40 in.). Private collection.

11. *The Exiles,* 2008. Oil on linen, 121.9 x 111.8 cm (48 x 44 in.). Collection of Peter and Mary Kane.

12. *The Dance,* 2003. Oil on canvas, 45.7 x 61 cm (18 x 24 in.). Private collection.

13. *The Oracle,* 2009. Oil on canvas, 111.8 x 116.8 cm (44 x 46 in.). Private collection.

14. *Pastors at the Gate,* 2008. Oil on canvas on wood, 61 x 304.8 cm (24 x 120 in.). Private collection.

15. *The Exchange,* 2007. Oil on canvas, 91.4 x 86.4 cm (36 x 34 in.). Private collection.

16. *The Guides,* 2004. Oil on canvas, 111.8 x 162.6 cm (44 x 64 in.). Collection of Paul and Susan Ward.

17. *The Inquiry* (detail), 2008. Oil on linen, 101.6 x 78.7 cm (40 x 31 in.). Private collection.

18. *Bathers at Dusk* (detail), 2007. Oil on linen, 91.4 x 121.9 cm (36 x 48 in.). Private collection.

19. *Overlook* (detail), 2007. Oil on canvas, 61 x 76.2 cm (24 x 30 in.). Collection of Wild Bill Jones and Dyann M. Lyon.

20. *The Reflection,* 2006. Oil on canvas, 121.9 x 162.6 cm (48 x 64 in.). Private collection.

Pomegranate Communications, Inc.
Box 808022, Petaluma CA 94975
800 227 1428   www.pomegranate.com

Distributed by Pomegranate Europe Ltd.
Unit 1, Heathcote Business Centre, Hurlbutt Road
Warwick, Warwickshire CV34 6TD, UK
[+44] 0 1926 430111
sales@pomeurope.co.uk

Color reproductions © Robert Bissell
Line drawings © Pomegranate Communications, Inc.

Catalog No. CB148

Designed and rendered by Susan Koop

Printed in Korea

22 21 20 19 18 17 16 15 14 13   10 9 8 7 6 5 4 3 2 1

2.

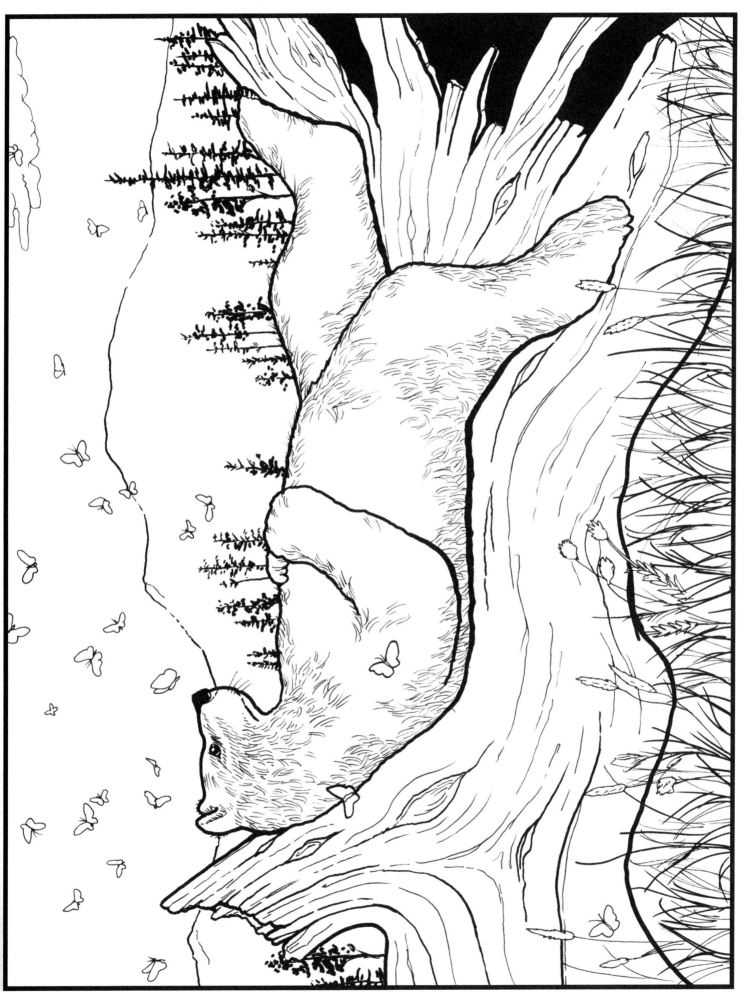

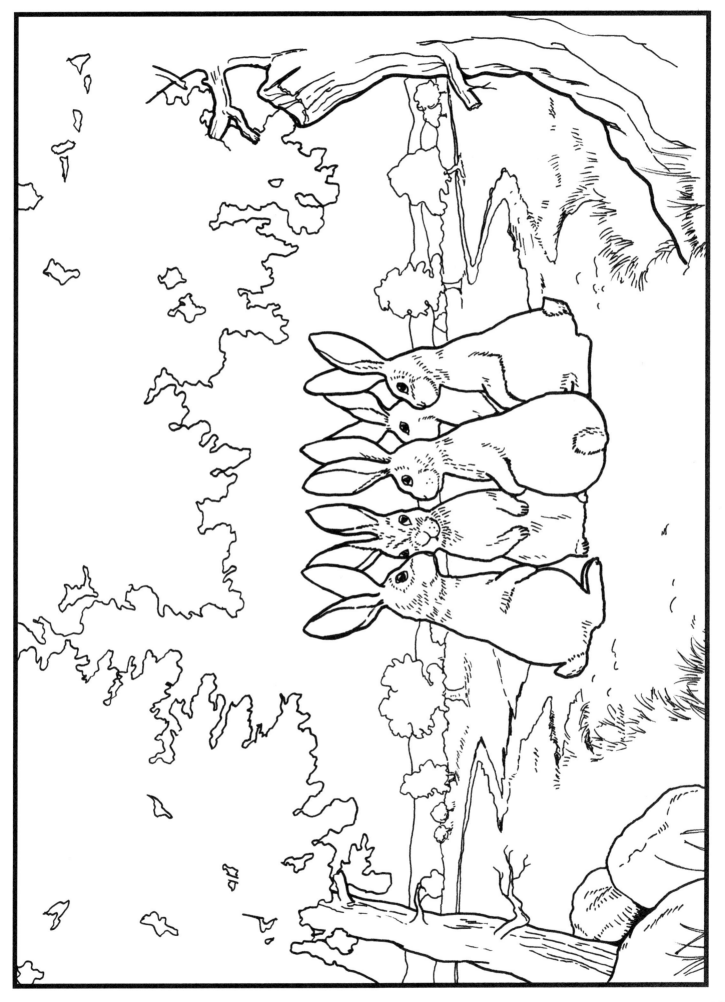

10.

11.

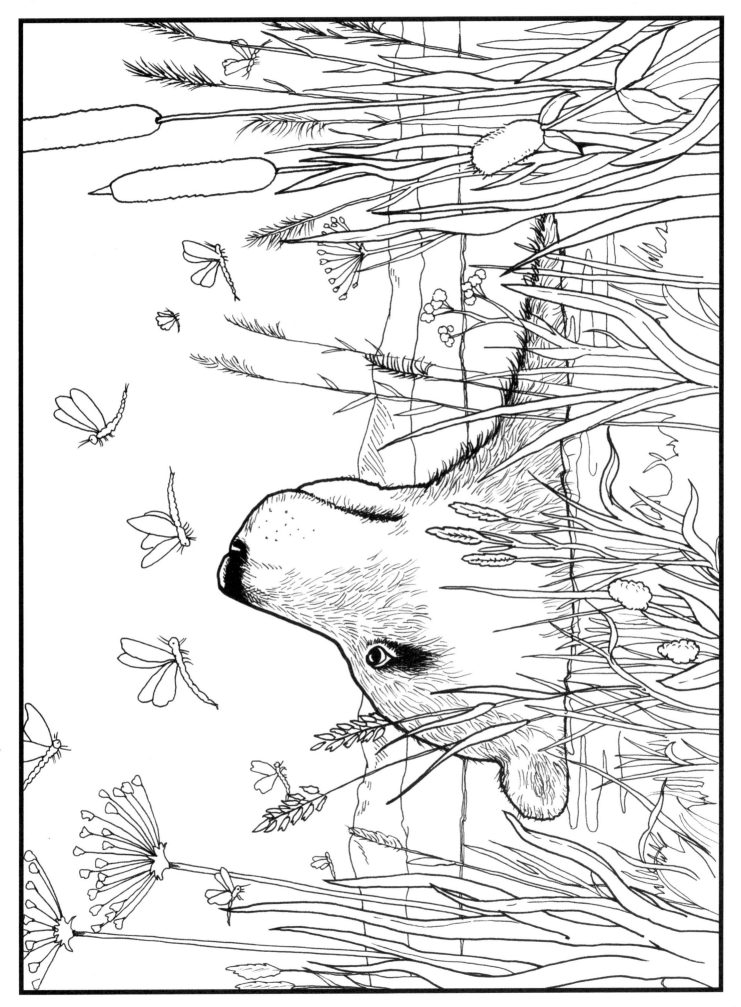

12.

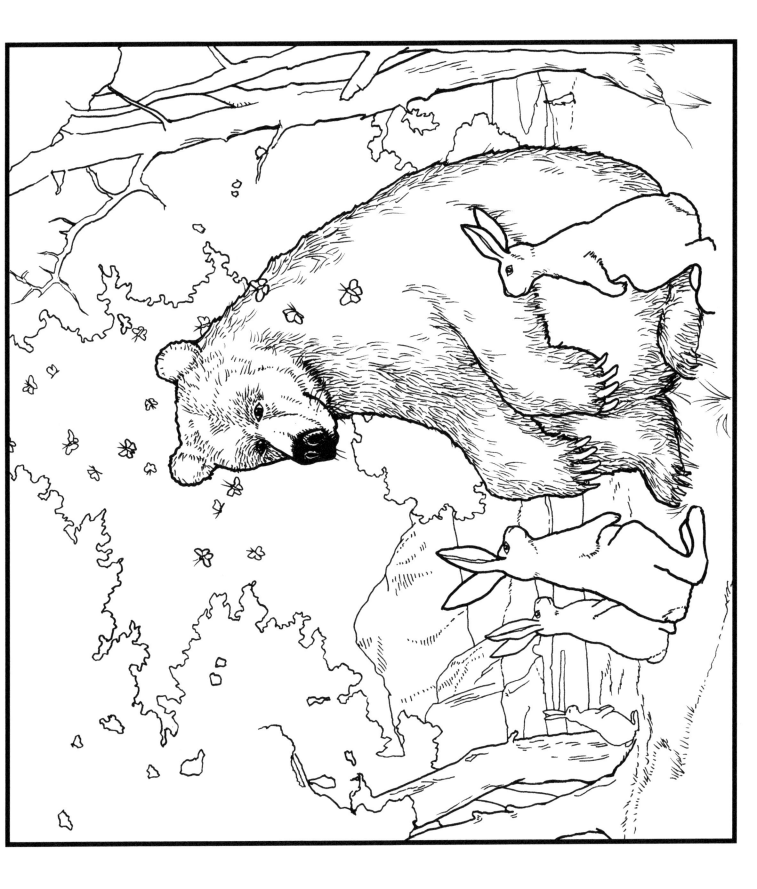

14.

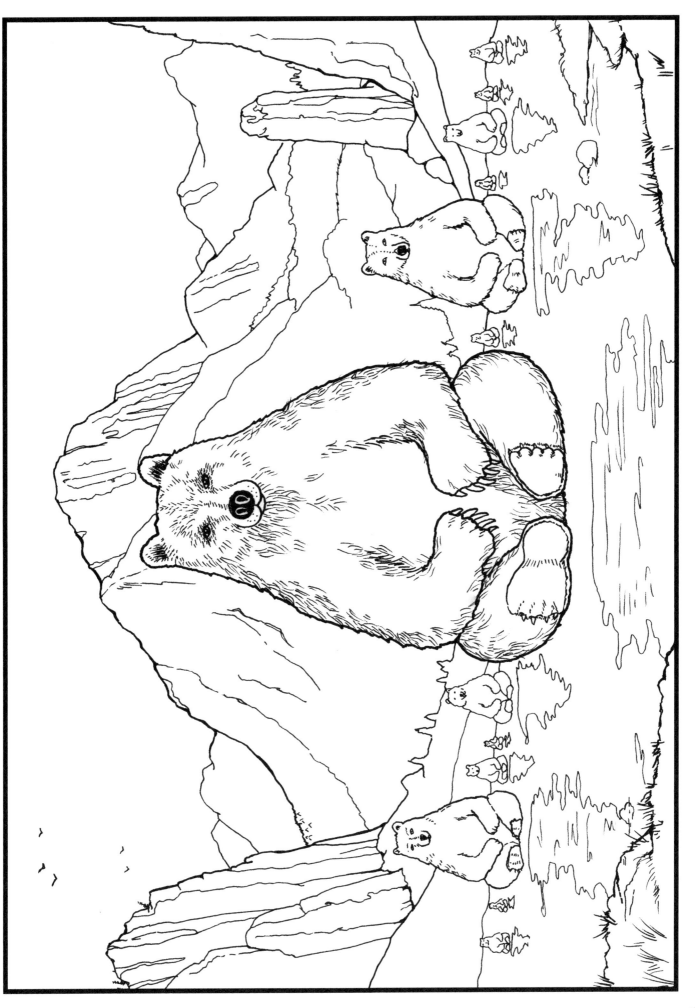

16.

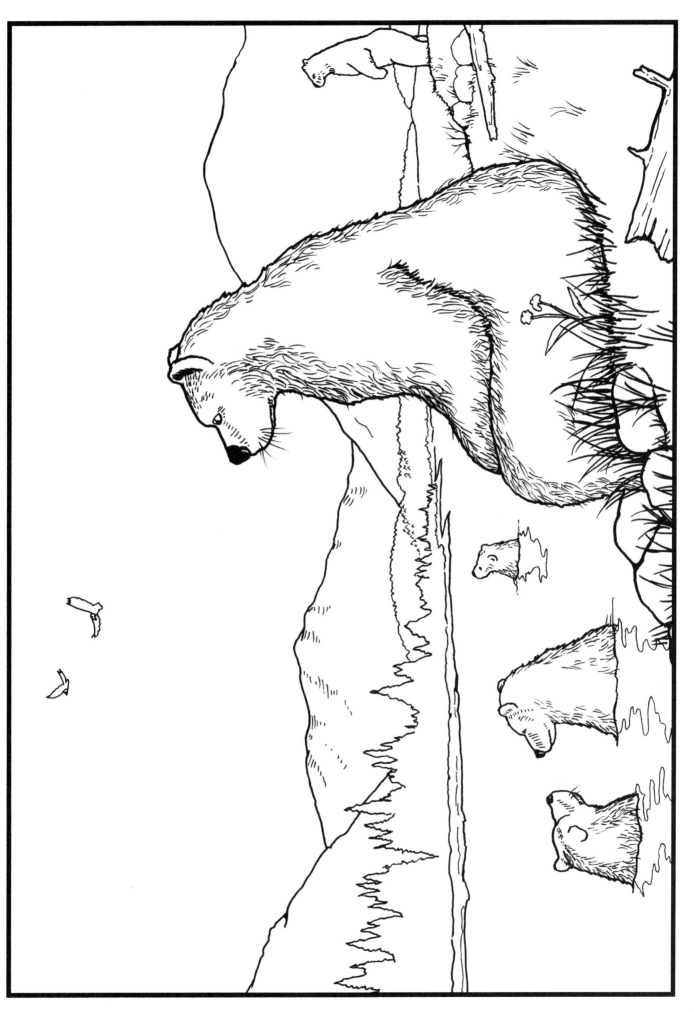

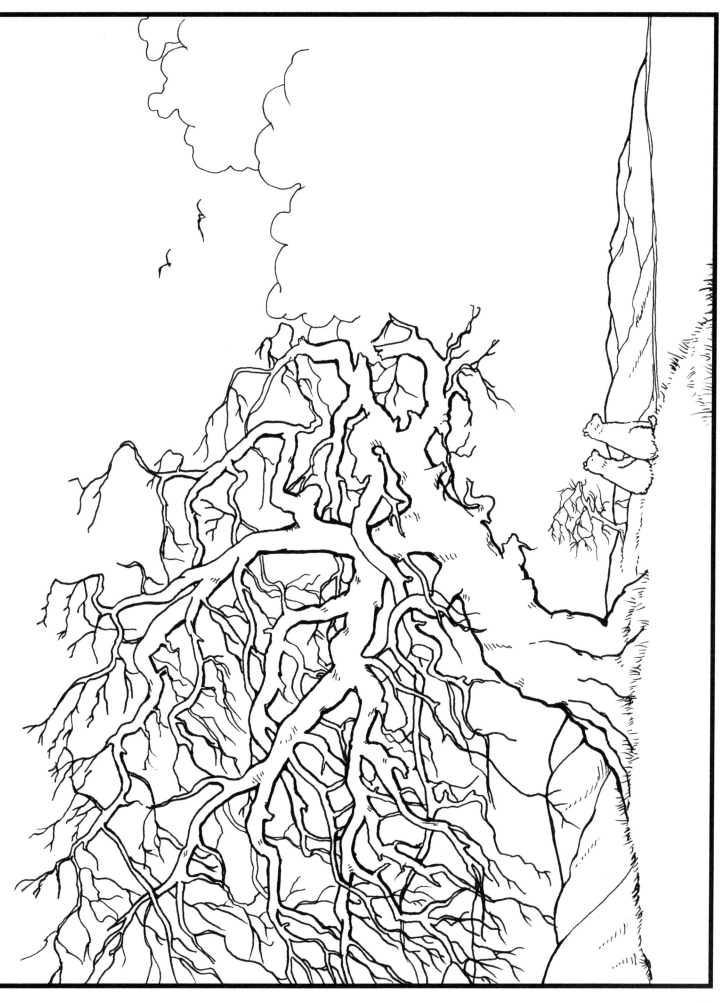

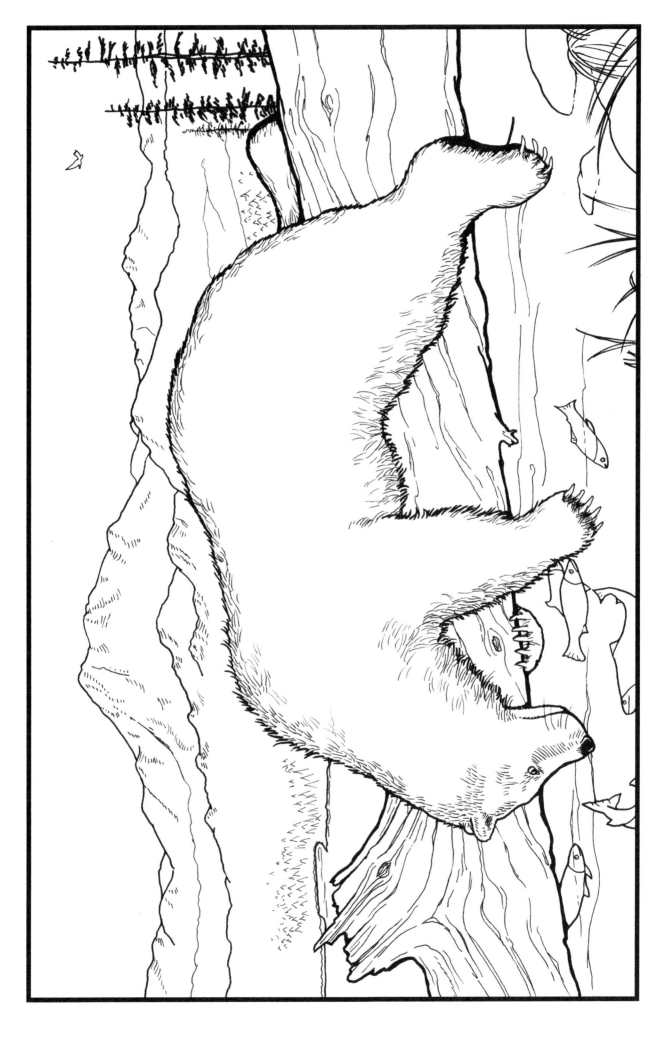

20.

Draw and color your own picture here!

Draw and color your own picture here!

Draw and color your own picture here!